I0493374

5s Lean Manufacturing
(Key to Improving Net Profit)

By Ade Asefeso MCIPS MBA

Copyright 2014 by Ade Asefeso MCIPS MBA
All rights reserved.

Second Edition

ISBN-13: 978-1499388015
ISBN-10: 1499388012

Publisher: AA Global Sourcing Ltd
Website: http://www.aaglobalsourcing.com

Table of Contents

Disclaimer

This publication is designed to provide competent and reliable information regarding the subject matter covered. However, it is sold with the understanding that the author and publisher are not engaged in rendering professional advice. The authors and publishers specifically disclaim any liability that is incurred from the use or application of contents of this book.

If you purchased this book without a cover you should be aware that this book may have been stolen property and reported as "unsold and destroyed" to the publisher. In this case neither the author nor the publisher has received any payment for this "stripped book."

Dedication

This book is dedicated to the hundreds of thousands of incredible souls in the world who have weathered through the up and down of recent recession.

To my family and friends who seems to have been sent here to teach me something about who I am supposed to be. They have nurtured me, challenged me, and even opposed me…. But at every juncture has taught me!

This book is dedicated to my lovely boys, Thomas, Michael and Karl. Teaching them to manage their finance will give them the lives they deserve. They have taught me more about life, presence, and energy management than anything I have done in my life.

Chapter 1: What is 5s?

5S is a simple and highly effective set of lean manufacturing techniques that removes waste from the work environment through a better workplace organization, general cleanliness and effective visual communication.

5S is the name of a workplace organization methodology that uses a list of five Japanese words which are seiri, seiton, seiso, seiketsu and shitsuke. Transliterated or translated into English, they all start with the letter "S". The list describes how items are stored and how the new order is maintained. The decision-making process usually comes from a dialogue about standardization which builds a clear understanding among employees of how work should be done. It also instils ownership of the process in each employee.

There are 5 primary traditional phases of 5S: sorting, straightening, systematic cleaning, standardizing, and sustaining. Lately, there are two other phases sometimes included, safety & security.

Sorting (Seiri)

Eliminate all unnecessary tools, parts, and instructions. Go through all tools, materials, and so forth in the plant and work area. Keep only essential items and eliminate what is not required, prioritizing things as per requirements and keeping them in easily-accessible places. Everything else is stored or discarded.

Straightening or setting in order / stabilize (Seiton)

There should be a place for everything and everything should be in its place. The place for each item should be clearly labelled or demarcated. Items should be arranged in a manner that promotes efficient work flow. Workers should not have to bend repetitively to access materials. Each tool, part, supply, or piece of equipment should be kept close to where it will be used in other words, straightening the flow path. Seiton is one of the features that distinguish 5S from "standardized cleanup". This phase can also be referred to as Simplifying.

Sweeping or shining or cleanliness / systematic cleaning (Seiso)

Keep the workplace tidy and organized. At the end of each shift, clean the work area and be sure everything is restored to its place. This makes it easy to know what goes where and ensures that everything is where it belongs. A key point is that maintaining cleanliness should be part of the daily work not an occasional activity initiated when things get too messy.

Standardizing (Seiketsu)

Work practices should be consistent and standardized. All work stations should be identical. All employees should be able to work in any station doing the same job with the same tools that are in the same location in every station. Everyone should know exactly what his or her responsibilities are for adhering to the first 3 S's.

Sustaining the discipline or self-discipline (Shitsuke)

Maintain and review standards. Once the previous 4 S's have been established, they become the new way to operate. Maintain focus on this new way and do not allow a gradual decline back to the old ways. While thinking about the new way, also be thinking about yet better ways. When an issue arises such as a suggested improvement, a new way of working, a new tool or a new output requirement, review the first 4 S's and make changes as appropriate.

Safety

A sixth phase, "Safety", is sometimes added. There is debate over whether including this sixth "S" promotes safety by stating this value explicitly, or if a comprehensive safety program is undermined when it is relegated to a single item in an efficiency-focused business methodology.

Security

A seventh phase, "Security", can also be added. In order to leverage security as an investment rather than an expense, the seventh "S" identifies and addresses risks to key business categories including fixed assets, material, human capital, brand equity, intellectual property, information technology, assets-in-transit and the extended supply chain.

It is important to have continuous education about maintaining standards. When there are changes that affect the 5S program such as new equipment, new products or new work rules, it is essential to make changes in the standards and provide training. Companies embracing 5S often use posters and signs as a way of educating employees and maintaining standards.

Chapter 2: What is Lean Manufacturing?

Defining Lean Manufacturing

Understanding what lean manufacturing is does not take rocket science, nor does it take a conference of ten experts to bear down to the basic concepts. Simply put, lean manufacturing is the achievement of the greatest efficiency and profitability for a company by eliminating the wasteful methods and activities that are commonly present in corporate regimes.

At first glance, some firms are intimated with the thought of adopting lean manufacturing because of its fancy sounding name. But, if truth be told, it is actually easier than seems. What you just need to have is the dedication and the discipline to see things through and make change happen.

Lean manufacturing is said to be a form of continuous improvement and when a company adopts it, a full-time continuous improvement person must be identified within the company as well as a continuous improvement team must be formed.

The company will then bring in a recognized expert with the organisation or a consultant to be able to map out the company's operation and help it identify specific areas for improvement.

First up, let us identify what the top seven wastes companies identified as the reasons for the production delays, gargantuan costs and, eventually, bankruptcy filings and hostile takeovers or merger.

1) Overproduction
2) Transportation
3) Motion (processes that don't need to be conducted)
4) Inventory
5) Processing
6) Waiting time
7) Defects

These are the key reasons why most firms often fail. For instance, with defects, instead of focusing on achieving the best quality output at the shortest period of time, some firms waste effort and energy into looking at and fixing equipment and method defects and problems. If the kink had been addressed in the first place and the problem nipped at the bud, such an unnecessary activity would be eliminated.

Definitions of popular lean manufacturing terms

If a company wants to fully understand what lean manufacturing is, it should first familiarize itself with some of the prominent technical terms linked to it. Do not let these words scare you off.

Cellular manufacturing

This involves the linking manual and machine operation to achieve the most efficient and cost-effective combination that would extract maximum value from a certain activity and method, while reducing wastes at the same time. Cellular manufacturing is usually U-shaped and flows in a single pattern.

Kanban System

This is a pull method that makes use of colour-coded cards attached to parts to be able to ensure the smooth flow of the production process. A 'pull method' simply means the customer's interest is foremost, instead of you as the manufacturer dictating what the consumer should have.

Value

This is what the customers are willing to pay for. It is the responsibility of the lean manufacturing strategy to deliver what the customer wants exactly.

Pull system

This involves the replacement only of goods that have been used up or depleted.

Takt time

This is identified by the customers' rate of demand. The takt time is what sets the production pace and matches it with how badly consumers need the product delivered to them. It is often referred to as the heartbeat of lean manufacturing systems!

In the end, what lean manufacturing is aiming to complete is the overall improvement of the company manufacturing process. The company manufacturing process has always been important part of an organisation that deserves to be continuously improved upon. Therefore, the last theme of a lean manufacturing system is continuous improvement. The lean manufacturing system has been an inspiration to other parts of company processes as well.

Chapter 3: Lean Manufacturing Principles

Understanding the Lean Manufacturing Principles

Companies are always searching for a more efficient way to run their business. Cost cutting is the most popular way of doing getting ahead of the competition. This ideal management setting can be achieved by practicing the lean manufacturing principles.

Lean manufacturing is the management philosophy of no waste. The focus is on reducing the seven wastes in the manufacturing business or any other type of business. The seven wastes are over-production, transportation, processing, waiting time, motion, inventory and scarp.

The lean manufacturing principles serve as the outline and guide for any company wanting to get the best out of their organization. The lean manufacturing principles are taken as the outline for making a more productive work environment, whether it is in a warehouse, factory or the office.

Perfect Time

The first of the lean manufacturing principles is the perfect first-time quality. This is a quest for having zero defects by revealing and solving the problems right at the source. By cutting all the wasted time during quality inspection at the end of the production process, efficiency is reached.

How does one achieve perfect first-time quality? By taking care of the problems at the source. Usually, after a thorough examination of how the usual production process is undertaken, the holes or inefficiencies of the process are exposed. After that, steps are taken to solve these holes immediately.

The end result of following the first of these lean manufacturing principles is that it reduces the time spent checking for product defects or organization faults because all the problems are addressed even before they can become a major problem for the company.

Get rid of waste

The second of the lean manufacturing principles is waste minimization. This preaches to eliminate all those activities or departments that do not add significant value and safety nets for the company. This means the resources of the company (people, capital and land) are put into better use.

Although this entails cutting off some workers, the option of reassigning them to departments where their talents can be utilized remains open. Often times, corporations, to justify mass lay-offs of their workers, use this second of the lean manufacturing principles. In reality, waste minimization is more effective when used in within the corporate hierarchy.

Never ending pursuit of the best

The third of the lean manufacturing principles is continuous improvement. As the title suggests, this principle focuses on continuous ways to improve the company. Finding the best way to do a task, reduce cost and improving product or work quality are examples of following this principle. At this point, any suggestions for improvement should be examined and, if proven to make the system more efficient, should be implemented at once. Information and tested knowledge govern the lean manufacturing principles.

Flex your muscles!

The fourth of the lean manufacturing principles is flexibility. This requires foresight from management and a keen sense of the market trend. Flexibility means producing a mix or diversity of products quickly without sacrificing quality, even at low volumes of productions.

How can these lean manufacturing principles be followed? By having a sound business plan at the start of the year and closely monitoring the market. The business plan should be flexible enough to adjust for any increase in volume or to make a new product in a short time. Expecting the unexpected and handling it with grace can sum up these lean manufacturing principles.

Pull not push

Pull processing is the fifth of the lean manufacturing principles. Simply put, pull processing means that the products are pulled from the consumer end, not pushed from the production end.

It's all about relationships

The last of the lean manufacturing principles dictates the importance of building and maintaining a good, long term relationship with the company's suppliers/partners through different management tactics like collaborative risk sharing, information sharing arrangements and cost sharing.

By doing so, your company and theirs will grow together. As odd as this last of the lean manufacturing principles sound, it is by working with these people that your organization will achieve greater efficiency and the possibility of more job opportunities with your suppliers or partners is heightened.

Following these lean manufacturing principles does not necessarily mean a leaner, more productive organization. Just as having the map is important, so is the execution of the lean manufacturing principles. The creation of a sound plan and firm implementation can make or break the effectiveness of these lean manufacturing principles.

Chapter 4: Lean Manufacturing Processes

Understanding Lean Manufacturing Processes

Empowering and inspiring firms to implement strategies that would seek the maximum value of their goods and services and, at the same time, reduce wasteful elements and activities significantly is the primary goal of lean manufacturing processes.

Since its introduction, most observers say it was pioneered by business tycoon Henry Ford and further developed into popularity by Toyota; every company has been intrigued by what lean manufacturing processes can do for their bottom-line.

For those firms that have already been implementing lean manufacturing programs, the method has been proven to be a huge benefit and success not just for the companies, but also for their respective workforces.

Lean manufacturing processes for the workforce

Employees, no doubt, are considered to be major elements of the manufacturing line. Workers benefit from the implementation of lean manufacturing processes because the work load is somehow eased and made less redundant.

The key principle of lean manufacturing processes is reducing and or eliminating waste in the corporate setting. One of the seven wastes the program identifies is waiting time. If employees see a reduced waiting time, they become more productive and more in-tune with their work environment. And a positive environment is what leads to the most positive results.

Lean manufacturing processes for the customers

Consumers will only willingly pay for something that will give them value for their money.

What lean manufacturing processes do is help give customers exactly what they want. The system helps manufacturers keep their customers best interests in mind and focus on their needs. The more customer-centric a company is, the happier its clients are.

To make this happen, firms conduct studies and surveys to find out what clients are looking for. It is through these that companies will be able to focus on the resources and energies available to achieve that need.

Lean manufacturing processes for the company itself

Companies will benefit greatly from this philosophy because it primarily seeks to reduce costs and achieve the best output without overdoing it. The term 'lean' says just that. Delivering the right goods, at the time right time, at the right place and in adequate quantities.

Thus, no excesses. No overproduction. No annoying stockpiles. If firms adopt lean manufacturing processes, they can be assured that nothing is wasted at any level of production.

Lean manufacturing has identified the seven wastes firms should eliminate if they want to achieve their fullest potentials:

- Transportation - inventory - waiting time - motion - defects - underutilized workforce, and - overproduction

These seven have been identified by companies all over the world as they key reason for unaccounted costs and weak production levels. These are what lean manufacturing processes aim to eradicate.

Critics say that lean manufacturing is costly at first, because major changes will need to be made to systems that have been in operation for decades. However, when you really think about it, what lean manufacturing expends at the preliminary stage is more than compensated for in the longer term.

Adopting lean manufacturing processes takes risks. But this does not mean that we are compelled to stick to age-old and obsolete methods just to be on the safe side, especially when we already know what this strategy can bring to the fore.

Chapter 5: The Five Principles of Lean Manufacturing

All companies seek ways to improve their businesses. One of the most common goals of trumping the competition is cutting expenses, which can be best achieved through lean manufacturing strategies.

But before anything, let us first define what lean manufacturing is. Lean manufacturing is a management concept that supports the 'no waste' policy. These 'wastes' refer to the seven most common reasons for under productivity and delay identified by companies all over the world.

They are inventory, over production, waiting time, transportation, processing, scrap and defects and motion. According to studies, most firms waste between 70% and 90% of the resources available to them. These happen when there are huge stockpiles of overruns, or when it takes ten activity levels to achieve something that can be done equally as good as when completed in three steps. The list can go on, but you get the picture.

The tricky part about implementing lean manufacturing principles is that most of the wastes identified are invisible, making their reduction and eventual eradication challenging. But with careful planning, lean manufacturing should be a walk in the park for your company

There are five core disciplines in lean manufacturing. Not all firms require their implementation, but at least one of which is necessary for the betterment, or 'leaning', of an organization.

1) Team development
2) Cellular manufacturing
3) Six sigma and total quality management
4) Rapid setup
5) Pull scheduling

To complement the above, the following five lean manufacturing principles are what serve as guidelines for firms that want to maximize value out of their organization.

Out With Waste

Lean manufacturing principles focus on eliminating waste from the company. This means taking out unnecessary departments or redundant positions, or eradicating processes that just cause delay.

If it means terminating jobs, then do so. Lean manufacturing espouses that all resources, land, persons and capital, are used in the best and most efficient way they can be used.

Do it Right the First Time

Trial and error methods are simply a waste of resources and time. If enough effort is placed in carefully planning a certain manufacturing process, then there would not be the need to start all over again, or settle with mediocre situations.

Always Seek the Best

Every company should always reach for the highest value that can be achieved. All the effort will be futile and major waste if this isn't done so.

Be Flexible

Lean manufacturing principles do not support stiff and linear thinking. If something needs to be improved and changed along the way, then do so at once, instead of contending with the original plan that has been eventually found to be resource and time-wasteful along the way.

Don't Push, Pull

Consumers should be given the freedom to decide what they want. As a manufacturer, you should impose trends or products to your clients. Rather, you should always be on the lookout for what will make your consumers happy.

Of course, adopting lean manufacturing principles does not always mean that your company is saved. It still takes careful planning, method-mapping and a lot of discipline to succeed. If your company is not wary of the consequences of strategies that are haphazardly implemented, then these lean manufacturing principles will be in vain and total waste.

Chapter 6: The Theory of Constraints and Lean Manufacturing

The theory of constraints and lean manufacturing are two of the most famous business beliefs that have made an impact to the business industry for years.

Though both popular in the business field, the theory of constraints and lean manufacturing are both similar in some aspects as they are in complete conflict in other views.

Listed below are some of the strengths of the theory of constraints and lean manufacturing:

1. The theory of constraints provides focus to the student in a world of information overload.

2. The theory of constraints provides its practitioners an opportunity to improve their organization by limiting their focus on very few issues which are the seen constraints to ongoing profitability.

3. The lean manufacturing on the other hand became famous after being derived from the system of the successful Japanese automobile maker Toyota. The lean manufacturing approach teaches that to improve the organization, a practitioner must focus on the elimination of any or all waste.

Listed below are some of the similarities of both the theory of constraints and lean manufacturing:

1. As is evident, the theory of constraints and lean manufacturing both focus on the improvement and advocate techniques to control the process flow of a material on the manufacturing shop floor.

2. The theory of constraints and lean manufacturing have both demonstrated impact results of implementations. That is, profitability skyrockets, as well as inventories and lead times are slashed and the operations are drastically simplified in both the theory of constraints and lean manufacturing.

3. Both the theory of constraints and lean manufacturing recognize that the perspective of the change agent must not be limited to the manufacturing part of the business but must echo throughout the rest of the company. This is in order to gain and maintain the improvement trends that both theory of constraints and lean manufacturing are focused on.

4. Both the theory of constraints and lean manufacturing are able to expand their scope in order to cover principles and practices of the entire business system. This will enable a continuous system-wide improvement for both the theory of constraints and lean manufacturing.

5. Both the theory of constraints and lean manufacturing embrace the concept of value. Both the theory of constraints and lean manufacturing are

two philosophies that agree that value is defined by the end customer.

6. Both the theory of constraints and lean manufacturing have an acknowledgement that the customer value is created by a chain of interdependencies that pushes far beyond the walls of manufacturing.

7. Both the theory of constraints and lean manufacturing also acknowledges that the work goal of every person in the business organization is to turn the inventory into throughput.

8. Both the theory of constraints and lean manufacturing observe defining the system and understanding the actual process flow as an early step.

9. Both the theory of constraints and lean manufacturing advocate the concept of the importance of flow.

10.Both the theory of constraints and lean manufacturing embraces the Pull principle while also offering methods of control to the flow of product that are based from the Pull principle from the market.

11. Both the theory of constraints and lean manufacturing agree that the business organization is focused on pursuing ongoing improvement. Both the theory of constraints and lean manufacturing agree that it is an endless pursuit of perfection.

12. Both the theory of constraints and lean manufacturing are also recognizing the importance of the workforce in participating in improving systems. It is noted by both the theory of constraints and lean manufacturing that it is the ownership of ideas together with the demonstrated results that ignites the flame of continuous improvement.

Listed below are the main difference between the theory of constraints and lean manufacturing:

1. Both the theory of constraints and lean manufacturing differ in how they focus their energies. The theory of constraints focuses on the notion to improve the system beginning with the current state of the system. The lean manufacturing, however, is bent on eliminating or reducing waste.

2. Both the theory of constraints and lean manufacturing differ in how the boundaries are defined in the value stream itself. The theory of constraints focuses on resources that are shared across value streams while lean manufacturing organizes itself around specific products.

Chapter 7: Learning the Basics of Lean Manufacturing and Processing

Lean manufacturing and processing has been an important strategy and basic technique in helping companies improve their profitability and competitiveness.

The fundamental function of lean manufacturing and processing is to reduce wastes and unnecessary work practices and behaviours among workers of a particular manufacturing company.

Because the times have really gone hard, demanding and intense due to political and turbulent concerns affecting all nations, firms are currently facing challenges to be able to keep their profitability and efficiency.

In principle, there are seven identified "forms of waste" within the work environment and systems that lean manufacturing and processing principally aims to alleviate, if not totally eliminate. These are over production, over processing, transportation, motion, inventory, waiting and scrap and defects.

Lean manufacturing and processing principles not only reduce operational costs but also aims to boost, restore and drastically improve the competitiveness of a troubled or struggling, even already good-performing, company.

31

That is basically why learning about lean manufacturing and processing has somehow become imperative for major and global companies.

The era of complete globalization is at hand. That contributes more pressure for companies to start acting right away to be able to survive the rough and hard operational and company challenges ahead.

Lean manufacturing and processing

Lean manufacturing and processing surely gets companies moving along and enjoying huge benefits of really reducing operational costs. If savings are generated, the saved amounts can be used for further capital requirements and investments that could further help companies expand and grow organically.

Lean manufacturing and processing, however, is not very easy to implement and adopt. The companies involved should really and religiously pay particular attention to details to be able to ensure the success of the efforts.

The number of companies adopting lean manufacturing and processing principles is surely and is apparently on the rise, no doubt about that.

But the thing is, firms adopting lean manufacturing and processing techniques are most of the time, not achieving target and aimed results because they are not doing the strategies and techniques properly.

Insufficient and ineffective implementation of lean manufacturing and processing principles and techniques will surely make the companies" efforts and capital infusion for the initiative futile and wasted.

It should be noted, also, that lean manufacturing and processing principles would not stand on its own. Companies adopting and embracing them should also strive harder to attain their goals.

Learn about lean manufacturing and processing

Experts advise companies to really get involved in and further learn more about lean manufacturing and processing. It is a logical and surely beneficial effort because lean manufacturing and processing can surely help companies get on with the current challenges and concerns affecting all firms around the world.

There are many ways on how companies can get to learn more about lean manufacturing and processing principles and techniques.

For one, they can hire lean manufacturing and processing experts and professionals who are credible and knowledgeable on the subject and who can really help the companies attain and maximize the benefits of such strategies.

However, hiring lean manufacturing and processing professionals will entail additional costs and investments from companies. They should not really mind it, because the benefits from lean manufacturing and processing implementation will surely offset the little and minimal costs of learning it.

Another thing, companies can designate key personnel to specifically and intently learn lean manufacturing and processing principles and techniques.

It is a common practice by companies around the world currently. The arrangement sees the key personnel attends seminars and get books to really know or learn the lean manufacturing and processing principles.

After that, the designated and assigned personnel will relay the message and everything he learned to the whole staff. It is up to him whether he will make the learning process for his officemates fast-paced or low-paced.

What is important is that the skills and knowledge are distributed and communicated to the entire organization. That way, lean manufacturing and processing principles are really and seriously imbibed by all personnel, to make the strategies work overall for the company.

Lean manufacturing and processing should be learned by all companies because the benefits it assures them, is nothing compared to the costs of absorbing them, which are not really that significant.

Wise, isn't it?

Chapter 8: When is Organizational Change Required by Lean Manufacturing?

Lean manufacturing has become a very popular and widely adopted economic and corporate management philosophy. Companies around the world are starting to turn to it amid political and economic crises even in the most progressive all nations.

Yes, the hard times have extended from the third world countries to the fully developed or first world countries. It is because economies are now led and influenced by volatilities involving oil producers and companies.

Because all industries are practically run and powered by energy, companies seem to not get away from the problems hounding the energy sector.

For almost more than a year now, firms around the world have been suffering from crunches brought about by the increasing and soaring prices of oil in the world market.

A lot of companies have fallen and have weakened due to the rising oil prices. There are more and more companies now filing for bankruptcy protection not because their management messed up or some executives defrauded them, but because of the external environment posed by volatile oil prices.

That is why, lean manufacturing is getting more and more attention, and more and more companies are deciding to finally implement the principles of the strategy.

Organizational change

Not because lean manufacturing is a strategy that initially and principally targets the structure of companies; lean manufacturing always commanding and demanding for organizational change.

Lean manufacturing aims to rationalize, streamline and accelerate corporate operations. But it does not mean organizational changes follow.

The organization is basically not altered or changed upon implementation of lean manufacturing principles. Lean manufacturing never targets organizational change, but instead hits changes in the organizations" environment design and work practices.

Organizational changes, however, are recommended and implemented along with lean manufacturing only when the desired results and outcome from lean manufacturing practices are not attained.

Failure of lean manufacturing is always found to be related to the effectiveness and adherence to the real principles in the implementation of lean manufacturing principles and strategies.

That is the only time when organizational change along with lean manufacturing is implemented. The effects and gains from the implementation will offset all the troubles and costs incurred, so why hesitate anyway?

Chapter 9: When is a Change in Management Required in Lean Manufacturing?

The Wikipedia Website defines lean manufacturing as a management issue or philosophy that focuses on the elimination, if not reduction, of the seven wastes.

The so-called seven wastes are identified by labour experts as the factors, both huge and little, that effect or influence the profitability of the given company.

You know that companies spend most of their capital on investments, equipment and work force. The investments are expected to generate revenues, which in turn decide on whether the company will keep afloat.

The seven wastes that companies find as burdens to their production and existence are defeats, motion, inventory, over processing, transportation, waiting time and over production.

A Gentle reminder of the seven wastes

As mentioned, the seven wastes are the usual factors that are blamed for the losses and demise of modern-day companies. The seven wastes, as you might have noticed, are somehow directly linked to the companies" working culture and environment.

Over production make up for filing of inventories, which is not necessary and negatively related to production because as supplies increase, prices do fall or decrease, as stated in the law of supply and demand.

Over processing and slow motion result in longer wasting time, which makes companies unproductive. Motion of personnel is disturbed and made slower when there lots of equipments not used in the workplace that obviously make free movement hard.

You know that when people can move freely, they can get to do more activities and accomplish more tasks.

Defects and scraps in outputs can be prevented along with all the wastes. The seven wastes also involve and cover behavioural patterns of employees, which can negatively affect the overall being of the company.

There are numerous advantages and benefits enumerated from the implementation of lean manufacturing principles.

For one, savings are consequently generated; revenues and incomes are rapidly and effectively improved. Savings will mean a lot to a company because capital is so hard to raise nowadays and operation factors and inputs are becoming more and more expensive.

Competition nowadays has also gone so intense that all companies, whether from different industries or not, are practically up against each other's" sleeves. Competitiveness is another aspect of the companies that lean manufacturing aims to cover.

To help cope up with the intense rivalry and competition among companies, lean manufacturing aims to boost production and quality credibility. These two factors are very essential when it comes to improving sales through active and good relations with customers and consumers.

The management and lean manufacturing

So one important question involving the adoption of lean manufacturing techniques is, "when is management revamped or changed resulting from the implementation of lean manufacturing techniques?

The answer to the question can somehow get hard and complex. To seek answers for the above mentioned interrogative statement would also be equally complicated and will require too thorough probing and searching.

Lean manufacturing principally aims to rationalize and streamline operations of companies. Experts argue that the process does not necessarily require a change in management.

But it can be noted that the distinct features of almost all companies under lean manufacturing initiatives are the change and revamp in management. The subject is the main cause of stress nowadays among executives and directors.

It can be safe and logical to assert, however, that because lean manufacturing entails the elimination of wasteful practices and behaviours in the workplace

41

that some executives are axed. It can be ironic that several board seats and top posts are only great wastes of capital and compensation packages.

I would recommend a change in management to most effectively make the adoption of lean manufacturing principles really work.

Chapter 10: Lean Manufacturing Ergonomics

Ergonomics is often referred to as a discipline containing human factors affecting or influencing manufacturing production.

Ergonomics mainly focuses on the human body, its capacity and its limits. Thus, ergonomics is often considered a full-scale scientific discipline that tries to touch and understand interactions between humans and other significant elements of a system, usually the working environment.

Thus, ergonomics as a profession aims to optimize well-being and total system performance of human beings working in an environment. To achieve that, ergonomics apply certain methods, data, principles and theories that would be of great significance to production.

Ergonomics and lean manufacturing

Lean manufacturing is a management principle or approach that principally targets the improvement in competitiveness and profitability of a business.

The main concern of lean manufacturing is to eliminate or scrap unnecessary and wasteful behaviour and practices of work personnel.

43

Thus, it would be safe and appropriate to say that lean manufacturing and ergonomics are bed mates. The two work disciplines and principles could greatly and undoubtedly complement each other.

It would also be proper to assert that ergonomics and lean manufacturing could work hand in hand to make sure the attainment of their respective goals and aims are achieved.

Ergonomics involve the design, assessment and evaluation of activities, tasks, workloads or jobs, products, working environments and work systems.

For its part, lean manufacturing involves approaches or business strategies that attempt to maximize productivity in the workplace by reducing, if not totally eliminating, unnecessary and unproductive tasks, activities and working behaviours.

Experts estimate that improvements brought about by adhering to ergonomics can bring in lean manufacturing results or save production time by as much as 25% to 40% on the general average.

Specific areas of lean manufacturing that targets lean manufacturing

There are five specific branches of ergonomics that can specifically bring in desired and productive results when integrated with lean manufacturing.

The five ergonomics branches are worker selection, man-machine allocation, anthropometrics,

44

biomechanics and physiology. Read on to find out more about these ergonomics branches.

Worker selection: Ergonomics suggest that to achieve a major streamlining initiative or lean manufacturing effort, companies should start from the top.

That means, to be able to eliminate and prevent wasteful and unproductive practices and behaviour in the office, they should hire personnel that are apparently able to contribute to maximized productivity.

Analysis of resumes and curriculum vitae of job applicants is very important, because the working nature of an individual are somehow stated within the contexts of these application papers. The employer should just learn how to read between the lines.

Man-machine allocation: Allocation in ergonomics and lean manufacturing means the division of work between personnel and machines or manufacturing equipment.

To be able to achieve this ergonomics goal, the management should carefully plan and assign the use of specific manufacturing machines by certain personnel. Through that, both the equipment and the worker are not worn out, thus, increasing productivity.

Anthropometry: Anthropometrics in ergonomics and lean manufacturing focuses on the human capacity. This branch concentrates and deals with the weight, dimension and strengths of the personnel's physical body.

By doing so, production will not be interrupted and smooth pacing of manufacturing is attained. Workers with weaker capacities will be assigned to handle works and equipments that they can surely handle, while the stronger workers will be given jobs using machines that fit their physical capacity.

Biomechanics: Like anthropometry, biomechanics in ergonomics and lean manufacturing deals with the human body, but this time, human movement and its mechanical forces are closely looked at.

In Biology, you know that motions and movements of the human body burn energy. By conserving body energy and allocating them for activities that will benefit production, manufacturing is boosted.

Physiology: Lastly, physiology in ergonomics and lean manufacturing deals with the anatomy of the human body. Designations and assignments of machines are done by first considering the physical structure of the workers" human body.

This time, it is not focused on certain body groups like muscles or energy requirements, but the whole body systems, from the physical, to the mental aspects.

Indeed, ergonomics and lean manufacturing are interrelated disciplines. Companies and firms that aim to maximize productivity should take the initiative to adopt and implement ergonomics and lean manufacturing strategies and processes.

Chapter 11: Lean Manufacturing in the UK

Lean manufacturing systems or processes are the process or system methodology of analyzing the method of flow of information or materials in a manufacturing environment. Using the lean manufacturing processes or systems also requires a continuous effort to improve the process itself to be able to achieve the enhanced value required by the company.

The Origination of Lean Manufacturing Process

The lean manufacturing in UK does not differ so much from other lean manufacturing in other countries. The lean manufacturing system or process that has evolved in North America was possible due to its origination from the lean manufacturing system or process of Toyota Production System in Japan.

This is a known fact and it is not farfetched that the lean manufacturing of UK has similar terms as the lean manufacturing of Japan or North America. A number of Japanese terms are incorporated on the lean manufacturing systems or processes in every country across the globe. Lean manufacturing terms such as kanban, and kaizen are definitely and arguably Japanese.

The lean manufacturing in UK similar to other lean manufacturing philosophies embraces a belief of excellence that includes the add-on of value and the elimination of waste or sometimes referred to as non-value added activities on the manufacturing system or process.

The lean manufacturing in UK also aims to monitor and adjust the existing production flow of the goods in accordance with the demand of the customer.

The lean manufacturing in UK uses the following as sort of building blocks to be able to operate its system and processes:

1. Standardized work is a method of the lean manufacturing in UK to make the work more synchronized and predictable which in turn delivers predictable and measurable results.

2. The lean manufacturing in UK also uses workplace organizations to be able to manage the flow and processes of work inside the company. Every looping or redundant process is seen as a hindrance to the improvement of the company's systems and processes.

3. The lean manufacturing in UK also uses visual controls to assure that the workplace and all its inherent processes are properly organized. Process flows and maintenance are very well adapted to visual controls so that employees can easily follow the proper work actions.

4. The lean manufacturing in UK also implements an effective plant layout which is a picture image of the manufacturing plant. The effective plant layout is

used to be able to find ways to further ease the process flow or manage a new configuration of the manufacturing equipment.

5. The lean manufacturing in UK also uses and observes quality at the beginning or source. This is possible by pre-emptive checking of resources and superior raw materials will definitely result to superior goods.

6. The lean manufacturing in UK uses batch reduction with the objective of reducing if not possibly eliminating the wastes that are present for each manufacturing batches.

7. The lean manufacturing in UK also forms teams or task forces to be able to meet deadlines or resolve matters by brainstorming and planning.

8. The lean manufacturing in UK is focused on customer demand-based manufacturing since the primary objective of lean manufacturing systems is to focus the energy and resources of the company towards the customer's needs and wants that are termed value.

9. The lean manufacturing in UK similarly uses a one-piece flow process. The one-piece flow process is essential to the easy monitoring and adjustments of existing manufacturing processes in a company. The one-piece flow process relies on the continuity of the manufacturing process and further automation and reduction of redundant processes will make the manufacturing system conveniently simple.

10. The lean manufacturing in UK also makes use of the takt time. The takt time is the demand rate of a customer. The takt time sets the pace of the manufacturing production so as to match the rate of every customer demand and subsequently becomes the heartbeat of any manufacturing system.

The takt time can be calculated by the division of the available work time by the total number of units that were sold.

Chapter 12: Move Ahead the Corporate Ladder with Lean Manufacturing Training

In a business setting that operates under lean manufacturing principles, it is important that the staff and employees of the company must have lean manufacturing training. Lean manufacturing is a management principle that almost every business wants to emulate. Lean manufacturing is all about reducing waste to make the business more effective and efficient.

Lean manufacturing training begins with the classroom setting with managers; consultant, implementers and employees are gathered to learn the concepts, formulate programs and create worthwhile solutions to the company's inefficiencies. The lean manufacturing training consultants may ask the staff to divide into teams.

Forming teams within the corporate system is very important in lean manufacturing training. Lean manufacturing philosophy depends on the correlation of the units is a large organization and the cause and effect of each person in the unit. When lean manufacturing training begins, the value of having team pride is expressed.

Teams undergoing lean manufacturing training cover a lot of areas from statistical Process Control, Team Building, Job Skills and Root Cause Analysis. Often during their training, many are shy and are reserved with their ideas. They lack the confidence in their work and do not really feel a part of something greater.

When they finish with their lean manufacturing training, all their inhibitions are set aside. Their lean manufacturing training makes them more competent in their jobs as a team and individuals. Giving these people a vision or attainable goal helps give them pride in them and their work.

During the lean manufacturing training, destructive and emotional conflict during work is turned into constructive brainstorming and problem solving. The lean manufacturing training sharpens the managers" decision-making abilities through case studies. Employees and managers see eye to eye on internal issues and their lean manufacturing training encourages them to think outside the box as a whole team when problems arise.

One of the major benefits of undergoing lean manufacturing training is the satisfaction of getting the job done. It gives pride to the team who solves it and helps make the company more efficient. By involving the entry-level staff to the managers in attaining realistic goals set within a timeframe, they are encouraged to give their best.

Another benefit is that the company stands to gain more from the lean manufacturing training. With the company's production processes becoming efficient without sacrificing the quality and quantity of the goods and services, more profits are expected to come in.

The lean manufacturing training also teaches the managers how to spot wastes within the system. Since zero waste is a must in the implementation of lean manufacturing, learning to identify what works and what doesn't in a department is a valuable trait for anyone wishing to climb the corporate ladder.

It is all about being smart and effective as an individual. Eventually, the door of opportunity will open once you have taken the lean manufacturing training to heart.

Lean manufacturing training for the different groups in a company

There are six groups that may be involved in the implementation of the lean manufacturing philosophy in a company. Because of the different level in the role of each group, lean manufacturing training for each of them also differs.

1. Executive Management: This group is responsible for establishing the culture of zero waste in all the departments. They are the ones everyone expects to set the bar for exemplary lean manufacturing training. Because of this, their training covers a lot of the philosophy of lean manufacturing and how to integrate its principles in the company's way of business.

2. Lean masters: This is a selected group of highly qualified company experts on lean management that are trained to become leaders in advancing the lean management plans. They are usually selected within the company and their lean manufacturing training is all about getting results.

3. Middle Management: This group is tasked with the responsibility of identifying opportunities within the company. They also must be able to prioritize which projects need more attention and how to achieve the results expected from the projects. Their lean manufacturing training is more focused on the production process of the company.

4. Lean Implementation Teams – this group is directly responsible for implementing the lean manufacturing tools throughout the organization. Their lean manufacturing training is requires them to have a good understanding of the lean tools to fulfil their directives.

5. Office Support – this group only undergoes lean manufacturing training when their actions can directly help in the success of the lean project. Often, they do not have to take the lean manufacturing training, but lean office!

With lean manufacturing training, everyone in the company can become a valuable resource. And by helping create a leaner more efficient workplace, the company can be expected to last for a very long time, which means more jobs and opportunities for promotion to its employees.

Chapter 13: Getting in Shape with Lean Manufacturing Techniques

Everyone wants to have a good physique and a healthy condition. When the entire body is working efficiently, the individual said to be strong and resistant to diseases. Training the body and toning the muscles can achieve this.

This analogy works in the business organization system. All departments work like the different parts of the body. When one is efficient and the others are lagging, the entire unit is not working at the optimum level. Lean manufacturing techniques can firm up the company by reducing wastes and making the organization better

Lean manufacturing is a management philosophy that concentrates on eliminating wastes and dividing the resources of the company into departments and business projects that requires the most immediate attention. The lean manufacturing techniques gives the company the opportunity to harness the best possible mix of all the best their organization can offer.

The first step in lean manufacturing techniques is to hire a lean manufacturing techniques consultant. Just like in a gym, a person hires a trainer to teach them the proper way to exercise, tone and sculpt their bodies. In the same way, companies must hire a lean manufacturing techniques consultant to guide them on how to achieve zero waste in the workplace.

Depending on the lean manufacturing techniques consultant and services that they offer, the standard process of training involves teaching the staff, employees and managers in a classroom setting. The concepts of lean manufacturing must be clear to these people in order for them to fully appreciate the benefits of streamlining their systems.

Lean manufacturing techniques involves analyzing the problematic parts of the organization, including the production department, making an assessment of the most inexpensive yet effective solution an implementing it to the organization.

Lean manufacturing techniques programs

There are different types of lean manufacturing techniques programs available to businesses. Some of these are:

1. 5S – This is a simple and highly effective set of lean manufacturing techniques that removes waste from the work environment through a better workplace organization, general cleanliness and effective visual communication.

5S means: Sort, Set in order, Shine, Standardize and Sustain. 5S lean manufacturing techniques program clearly positions the methods within the framework of the principles of lean manufacturing and the improvement of values in the organization.

The core of this 5S lean manufacturing techniques program is that to achieve an easy flow of products or services in the company in small groups, cleanliness and a followed set of procedures is needed.

2. Hoshin Kanri – This type of lean manufacturing techniques makes an aligned team. It makes employees feel part of the development of the system. Because of this, the smaller units of the corporation help higher management achieve goals more effectively as new kaizens are identified and implemented, all consistent with the vision and strategy.

3. Kaizen – This type of lean manufacturing techniques is applied as a part of the system level approach to improvement. A Kaizen event, also known as Kaizen Blitz, is focused; more intense short-term project that is made to improve the process of a certain department.

Kaizen events takes companies away from the traditional lengthy projects where valuable time and money is spent more on planning rather than making actual changes in the company.

4. Kanban – This is a type of lean manufacturing techniques focuses on the pull system of an organization. Kanban represents the visual aspect of the physical storage locations in the retail business.

Kanban and Supermarkets work hand in hand to establish and maintain the interactive relationship of the products from the customer back to the producer and to the suppliers. Lean manufacturing techniques explain the kanban scheduling systems that makes a more efficient way of stocking the goods from the warehouse to the point of purchase.

5. Set-Up Reduction (also known as Single Minute Exchange of Die or SMED) – This is a lean manufacturing techniques system that is often ignored. When the company doesn't have standard or set of procedures to follow on the start of any working activity, time is wasted. Lean manufacturing techniques flexes this attribute by effectively allowing employees to get used to a system and then do it frequently for more efficiency.

There are only a few of the lean manufacturing techniques program available to any business. Six Sigma training, value stream mapping, lean assessment, lean accounting and standardization of work are among others.

Get a leaner and more effective company by undergoing lean manufacturing techniques. You will have no regrets with the number of benefits this training system can do for your organization. If you need help on lean manufacturing training or implementation, feel free to contact us via this link. http://www.improvenetprofit.aaglobalsourcing.com/contact

Chapter 14: Getting the Most from the Tools of Lean Manufacturing

Lean manufacturing espouses the 'no waste' philosophy in managing the workplace and production processes. It does not know any company size. Whether it is a major corporation or a small group of five housewives with a cookie business, successful lean manufacturing techniques lies in its implementation and the discipline of those participating in it.

Experts say that lean manufacturing tools first gained popularity in Japan; a country best known for its highly unique and innovative approaches to a variety of things and methods, even with problem-solving strategies.

The success of lean manufacturing is determined by how implementing companies deal with and initiate ways to achieve maximum benefits from the resources available to them without having to spend too much. Success is also driven by the reduction and eventual elimination of the so-called wastes of corporate environments.

These wastes have been identified as: transportation (the movement of goods more than what is minimally needed), motion (employees working more than what is minimally required), defects (the efforts linked with inspecting and fixing problems), processing

61

(conducting more work than what is actually needed), overproduction (leading to wasteful stockpiles) and inventory.

It is a fact that all firms need to reduce costs, what with rising energy prices and intensifying competition. Reading business journals, you can see that firms are filing for bankruptcy left and right, citing mismanagement as the most common cause of the Chapter 11 filings in the US. Even the most stable companies have fallen prey to these. This is why lean manufacturing is starting to become the overhaul method of choice for firms wanting to get back on track.

The tricky part about implementing lean manufacturing tools is that most of the wastes identified are invisible, making their reduction and eventual eradication challenging. But with careful planning, lean manufacturing tools should be a walk in the park for your company

The following five lean manufacturing tools are what serve as guidelines for firms that want to maximize value out of their organization.

The Right Way, the First Time

Trial and error methods are simply a waste of resources and time. If enough effort is placed in carefully planning a certain manufacturing process, then there wouldn't be the need to start all over again, or settle with mediocre situations.

Go Away, Waste

Lean manufacturing principles focus on eliminating waste from the company. This means taking out unnecessary departments or redundant positions, or eradicating processes that just cause delay.

If it means terminating jobs, then do so. Lean manufacturing espouses that all resources, land, persons and capital, are used in the best and most efficient way they can be used.

In Constant Search for the Best Quality

Every company should always reach for the highest value that can be achieved. All the effort will be futile and major waste if this isn't done so.

No Pushing

Consumers should be given the freedom to decide what they want. As a manufacturer, you should impose trends or products to your clients. Rather, you should always be on the lookout for what will make your consumers happy.

Exercise Flexibility

Lean manufacturing tools do not support stiff and linear thinking. If something needs to be improved and changed along the way, then do so at once, instead of contending with the original plan that has been eventually found to be resource and time-wasteful along the way.

Chapter 15: Lean Manufacturing Systems

The lean manufacturing system is a general term applied to the latest methods of manufacturing that maximizes value and minimizes the waste. Lean manufacturing systems are varied systems designed to improve the manufacturing line of any company.

Definitions of Terms in Lean Manufacturing Systems

1. Value in terms of the lean manufacturing systems is basically what the customer is ready to pay for. A company will have to find out or survey what the customer really needs and then focus all its energies and resources towards that valued goods.

2. Waste in terms of the lean manufacturing systems is the opposite of the value. Everything that is outside the value that was assigned to a particular goods is deemed a waste. Anything that the customer is not willing to pay for is also deemed a waste.

The elimination of this waste can easily manifest itself in at most eight different categories:

a. Overproduction

Overproduction in lean manufacturing systems is the production of a particular good in higher levels and number than what is needed. When a customer orders a particular good, a company will have to manufacture it and deliver it on time.

The problem transpires when the company overproduces the goods and upon delivery, the customer will only buy what he needs. What is left of the products is then deemed as wastes since its quality has diminished and the customer is not willing to pay for it.

If a company has lean manufacturing systems, then it will be able to monitor how much it should produce and avoid overproduction.

b. Inventory

A problem in inventory arises when the stock is less than the demand by the customers. If a customer will not be able to get what he wants then it will be a bad image for the company.

Lean manufacturing systems can be administered to be able to avoid the untimely depletion of stocks by proper inventory. Once the stock is near depletion it must be replenished.

c. Defects

Correcting defects have always been a part of lean manufacturing systems. Lean manufacturing systems desire to decrease defects in the manufacturing line by improving processes and applying automation in specific points along the manufacturing line.

Defects are sometimes seen as caused by human errors but these defects can also be caused by improper machineries.

d. Extra processing

Extra processing based from lean manufacturing systems are processes that are seem to be redundant in the system. Extra processing can be solved by lean manufacturing systems simply by monitoring and identifying what specific processes are not needed anymore by the manufacturing line.

What the lean manufacturing systems are doing is to cut down unnecessary processes and improve the manufacturing line.

e. Waiting time

Waiting time per lean manufacturing systems is the unnecessary time that is spent and wasted along the manufacturing line. Again whatever process or loops that can be avoided by the lean manufacturing systems is implemented.

f. Underutilized people

Underutilized people are also part of the concern of lean manufacturing systems. Lean manufacturing systems finds proper solutions to be able to solve the problem of underutilized people.

Automation processes implemented along the manufacturing lines have induced the decreased need for people.

g. Motion

The motion of the manufacturing line is also a concern for the lean manufacturing systems. The processes of the manufacturing line must be streamlined and improved and lean manufacturing systems have drafted solutions to cut down unnecessary processes.

h. Transportation

The lean manufacturing systems also have a concern over the transportation wastes that a manufacturing company will incur. The lean manufacturing systems have eliminated a few of the problems by centralizing manufacturing operations per plant so that each plant can act and manufacture on their own.

3. Benefits of the lean manufacturing systems are many that include a better lead-time, more flexibility and more increased sales.

The internal influence of the lean manufacturing systems is the reduced space of operation and a progress in the work. Aside from improvements of quality and almost minimal expenditures.

Aside from this, lean manufacturing systems can benefit the company with a scrap reduction of about 90%, reduced set-up and lead times by about 90%

and 50%. Using lean manufacturing systems, companies can achieve about 20 inventory turns per year.

Chapter 16: The Benefits of a Lean Manufacturing System

A lean manufacturing system is a system and philosophy that was first developed by Toyota for its production system. Lots of manufacturing business has adopted this system for them to enjoy the benefits that it has to offer.

The name "lean manufacturing system" is a generic term that refers to the principles and theories to rid your business of waste. Waste in a lean manufacturing system is referred to processes that do not add to the value for money for the customer that buys from you.

The lean manufacturing system principles are:

1. Value - Customer's willingness to pay for your product.

2. Value Stream – Add-ons to a product or process.

3. Flow - The movement of your product being biased to single piece flow or work cells rather than production lines.

4. Pull - Having the right amount of materials to manufacture the product at the same time having a small or no inventory.

5. Continuous Improvement - Getting rid of waste on a constant basis.

For example, if you order a computer over the Internet it may take a week for your computer to be delivered to you. It will only take a few hours for the technician to assemble and have your computer ready for use.

The reason why it may take a week is because of the different shipping practices used by the company. It may also be bottlenecks within their current manufacturing system like having the company wait for the required materials to arrive that make you wait those extra days.

Having a lean manufacturing system for your business and the application of its various principles can make your order for a new computer shorter. Instead of waiting for a week for your computer to be delivered to you, it may just take 24 to 48 hours. The lean manufacturing system is designed to give the customer value for money at the lowest price at the least given time.

Another good example of a lean manufacturing system is the eyeglasses in an hour. Usually it would take at least 24 hours for glasses to be made and delivered to the customer, maybe even longer. A lot of lean principles have been applied to this lean manufacturing system. Now you see a lot of eyeglasses in an hour stores from malls to stores near your street.

Judging from the examples above you may think that the quickness in delivery is the only benefit that a lean manufacturing system can give a business. Actually this is just one in the many benefits that having a lean manufacturing system can offer. A lean manufacturing system also gets rid of waste while maintaining low cost and at the same time satisfying customer needs.

Getting rid of waste and all the useless processes is so crucial to the lean manufacturing system that it even has its own term 'muda." "Muda" in lean manufacturing system is also a Japanese word for waste.

There are seven types of considered waste in the lean manufacturing system which I have discussed in earlier chapters therefore I will on give a short description for completeness.

1. Over Production - Producing a product that is made faster than is sold is wasteful.

2. Inventory - A product that has to be stored is wasteful because it ties up money as inventory.

3. Conveyance - Moving a part unnecessarily during production is wasteful. Can also damage the parts.

4. Correction - Having to inspect, correct your products because of production errors is a huge waste of time and money. This can be overcome with error proofing. This means that the product can be made through that way only.

5. Motion - Awkward movements of the operator can put different aches on different parts of their body.

Making this area better will reduce injury and workman injury claims.

6. Processing - Customer requirements that are not clear to the manufacturer cause the manufacturer to produce different add-ons that is wasteful since it will increase the cost of the product.

7. Waiting - The operator doing nothing is a waste. It's ok that the machine waits for the operator not the other way around.

Eliminating waste through lean manufacturing system streamlines your company thus by getting more done with less equipment, capital, space, effort, labour, inventory and time.

Having a lean manufacturing system established in a company's organization could do wonders. This is because while saving time, money and precious resource, the company's production system is improved and becomes more efficient. Other companies admire this attribute that to have a lean manufacturing system can only mean a good management.

Chapter 17: Lean Manufacturing Implementing

Before we discuss how to implement the much discussed corporate planning strategy known as lean manufacturing, let us first define what it is again just as a reminder!

Lean manufacturing is a combination of approaches that, when put together, aims to eliminate all the common practices that are seen as wholly unnecessary and time-consuming. Such are called wastes, like overproduction, long waiting times, transportation and constant motion, which not only eat up precious time but are also a drag on resources, energy and expenses.

Simply put, implementing lean manufacturing has the reduction of costs in mind. And this is done, ironically, by first making sacrifices on the strategies that have been in effect in many companies for decades now.

Sound like a dangerous plan? Some companies believe it is, but when you really look at its long term benefits, you will find that implementing lean manufacturing will bring greater value to your company than the processes that have already been ingrained. After all, change is often for the better. You just have to open your eyes and welcome it.

Implementing the lean manufacturing program is best for companies that have output and production as their primary source of revenue. Such companies place a prime on maximizing their entire human and tool resources in order to achieve their target output levels without having to spend too much.

This is where the principles of lean manufacturing are most helpful:

Prevailing economic conditions often leave companies scampering for clients. Growing competition are forcing producers to lower their charges just to be able to get ahead, that is why such firms are looking for novel ways to lower their production costs and increase turnaround times. When firms need to boost efficiencies and generate revenue, lean manufacturing is often what is implemented.

Implementing lean manufacturing techniques has been found effective in the survival and success of a company or an organization. This is because of the 'elimination of seven wastes' philosophy this program espouses.

Lean manufacturing aims to teach and deliver products on-time, at the right time and at the right quantity approach to production. For instance, producing too much than what is needed is often detrimental to a company. Sure, it shows that targets have not only been achieved, but grossly surpassed. But this does not always entail success.

Implementing lean manufacturing systems means that there should be no waste. That is, no unnecessary stockpiles that could just sit at warehouses and left to rot. If you produce more than intended, this is what will likely happen to your inventory.

You will take up warehouse space and see the products get worn by time. If you are lucky, you will be able to dispose of the excesses, but they won't likely be sold at their original price because, well, they will be considered old stocks or overruns.

Before you plan to implement lean manufacturing strategies, it is best to be prepared. Critics are not kidding when they say that lean manufacturing is somewhat tricky, because the preliminary preparations can, indeed, deter you from pushing through.

The goal of lean manufacturing for any business is to have production and demand linked directly. The result is a more efficient way in delivering your goods to the customer because you produce the product at the time the customer wants it. But this is only achieved if there is a proper implementing lean manufacturing guideline.

However, despite the training and guidelines, some companies have trouble in implementing lean manufacturing systems. There are different reasons in the failure of implementing lean manufacturing principles in projects. One of them is the difficulty in grasping the true nature lean manufacturing.

The most accepted form of implementing lean manufacturing is the kaizen. Kaizen in Japanese means, "Improvement." In implementing lean manufacturing, kaizen can be done in large scale or small-scale projects. The most commonly used kaizen are the blitz events. These are short-term programs launched to instantly improve the production process.

Though kaizen is highly prized as a valuable tool in implementing lean manufacturing in a company, it is not enough. If an endless cycle of kaizen events is the only form of lean manufacturing tool used, the company may suffer. Why? Because blitz events can be expensive and may cost the organization more money in implementing it.

There are other implementing lean manufacturing tools that an organization can use to get the improvements they want. There is the Value Streaming and Process Mapping. These two can effectively eliminate waste and in implementing lean manufacturing, they can streamline work processes.

Although lean manufacturing may sound simple enough, there are companies that do not view it that way. They find implementing lean manufacturing obscure and cloudy. This means that they do not fully grasp the principles of lean manufacturing. The best solution is to hire a lean manufacturing consultant.

Once the consultant has made an assessment of the organization's problem areas, he can then suggest the most appropriate projects that will achieve the goals of the company. While the implementing lean manufacturing systems are explained to the managers and lean masters, the process of enforcing these systems and plans fall on the latter's shoulders.

For the company to fully appreciate the benefits of implementing lean manufacturing systems, they must be willing to wait. Change does not happen overnight and some resistance should be expected from the people directly affected by the implementing lean manufacturing systems.

Why is there resistance when lean manufacturing aims to improve the production quality of the organization? Simply put, some people hate change. They have been doing the same thing and have been used to going through the routine for years that it has almost become something familiar to them.

In light of this, companies should make it a point to clearly explain the changes in implementing lean manufacturing systems. If all things go smoothly for the first run, the implementing lean manufacturing system must be adopted as soon as possible to make sure that the workers do not forget the new process.

When implementing lean manufacturing systems involving the executive management, it is important to note that this group is the one that must have a full understanding of lean manufacturing principles. Their training must cover all disciplines of lean manufacturing including the planning and implementation tools.

Although lean manufacturing is one of the best choices for improving a company or organization, you must be certain if your business fits this philosophy. Not all implementing lean manufacturing systems may be good for your business, like excessive use of the kaizen events.

In implementing lean manufacturing systems, most often the best way to employ its principles is by only taking the elements that fit your company. This way you also save money without losing valuable resources.

However, consider the long term gains you will obtain from this system. If you list pros and cons, you will find that the benefits will significantly outweigh the tedious preparations and planning by a long shot. Once you have laid down what needs to be changed and what needs to be eliminated, implementing should be a piece of cake. Good luck!

If you need help on lean manufacturing training or implementation, feel free to contact us via this link. http://www.improvenetprofit.aaglobalsourcing.com/contact

What Makes a Successful Lean Manufacturing Implementation?

Choosing to apply lean manufacturing principles inside your company's organization is one of the smartest moves for any manager wanting to get ahead in the business. In today's competitive world, being one step ahead of everyone else is a major advantage.

Lean manufacturing can be the turning point for any organization.

Many companies who have tried lean manufacturing have experienced production growth of up to 25%, cost reduction from key areas of the organization and have developed a more personal relationship with the company as an identity. This is due to an effective lean manufacturing implementation plan.

Lean manufacturing implementation planning begins with the executive management. After laying down the departments and areas in production that needs immediate attention, planning for the lean manufacturing implementation begins. Depending on the gravity of one point, say cutting production time to 10%, the steps for achieving it is listed down.

Creating a planning for the lean manufacturing implementation in a department can be very useful. You can measure the success of the lean manufacturing implementation in quantifiable terms like percentage growth in production time or the cut in production time to meet the predetermined goals of the company. Phases of a lean manufacturing implementation plan

For lean manufacturing implementation to work, it has to run in phases within the company. The first phase is Core Disciplines. It requires all the concerned employees and managers to undergo lean manufacturing training. Once they have grasped the concepts and principles of lean manufacturing, they can now make plans for the lean manufacturing implementation in their departments.

When people understand what is required of them to become active members of a unit (the company, in this case), cooperation is easy to achieve. That is why the changes experienced in Phase one of the lean manufacturing implementation are usually dramatic, its results are immediate and the benefits are clear.

Phase two of the lean manufacturing implementation builds on the core disciplines. This means whatever changes have been implemented on the first phase; it is fine tuned in the next one. Systems are placed, as a permanent part of the organization's routine and training for sustaining those systems is an ongoing process.

The last phase is called Continuous Improvement. After the lean manufacturing implementation throughout the organization, the improvements made by the new systems gradually become part of the production process. The improvements may be small but as the months go by, it builds up like compound interest.

Phase three of the lean manufacturing implementation never ends. As long as the plans for lean manufacturing implementation are followed, the company will continue to feel the positive effects of the change. This will mean additional profits for the company through money saved from the cost reductions.

Keys to a successful lean manufacturing implementation

Depending on how effective the plans for lean manufacturing implementation have been to the specific department, there are still a few considerations to take for the plan to be successful.

First is prepare and motivate people. Quality training and recruiting of workers with appropriate skills can help lead an organization to lean manufacturing implementation success. The creation of teams to instil pride in one's work and organization is very good tool to get the people involved and really care about the company's growth.

Second, share information with the concerned people or those who are directly affected with the kaizen events and manage expectations by making the goals realistic. When people see that they are part of something important, they become empowered and it makes the lean manufacturing implementation a whole lot easier.

Third is to make an atmosphere of experimentation possible for any person in the organization. Small, calculated risks are allowed but major mistakes may cause the company to close down. It is important to draw the line of between honest mistakes from a corporate blunder.

Fourth is to install realistic performance measures, fair evaluation, and solid reward systems. When everything is manageable, the workload is eased and there are more opportunities to reward good performance.

The success of lean manufacturing implementation rests on the hands of the cooperation of the people inside the corporation. All you need to do is tap into their potential as a major resource and you have got it made.

Chapter 18: Adapting Lean Manufacturing

Lean manufacturing espouses the philosophy that the seven major wastes in every production process and company should be significantly reduced or even eliminated in order to be able to compete more effectively and dramatically boost profitability.

Times are changing fast and the demands of the market for faster delivery periods, higher quality and lower costs are placing huge tolls on every firm. This is where lean manufacturing comes in. What it does is help your firm rise up to the competition by being 'lean', that is, by taking out all the unnecessary activities and methods that cause problems and delay.

Lean manufacturing has identified seven major 'wastes', as named by companies surveyed all over the world: over processing, transportation, waiting time, over production, motion, scrap and defects and inventory.

For example, a certain production level becomes a huge waste of time, effort and resources if it's being done in ten levels, while it can be completed in just three.

Citing another case, productivity could have been raised if defects of a particular equipment or system had been addressed before processing began. A lot more could have been done you had not waited for it to bog down in the middle of everything and cause annoying delays.

Another one is where your company has overproduced and have no more space to stock the overruns. Where do you put the excesses? How do you manage to sell them? More likely than not, you will be forced to offload them at a price much lower than intended just so you could make room for new goods. And, this, as lean manufacturing says (and any businessperson would say) is major waste.

Studies show that firms adopting the lean manufacturing principles have seen that their productivity has gone up 75% to 125%.

This is because the energy and time usually spent on regular processes have been significantly lowered to allow for greater focus on quality and on what the customers truly need. With lean manufacturing, there is no 'this will have to do' attitude.

Everything is done at the right quality, at the right quantity, at the right time, all the time.

As with the workplace setting, lean manufacturing's focus on eliminating unproductive activities and tasks will also help the firm and its employees give more attention to what their clients need. No job will be haphazardly done because enough time is afforded to each level to make sure things are running smoothly.

When customer satisfaction is achieved, it follows that revenue will rise. Your client is happy, your company is happy, everybody is happy.

Lean manufacturing also aids the organization by weeding out redundant positions, thereby cutting labour costs and eventually raking in savings. It helps firms focus just on what needs to be done and do away with unwanted stress, especially those that arise from having too many people on board. With lean manufacturing, less is definitely more.

One major change that your company will see once you have adopted lean manufacturing concepts is the raised discipline among your employees. Because the culture becomes standardized, annoying kinks and practices are done away with.

While several people criticize lean manufacturing, saying it is a costly endeavour, you must be aware that the costs related to its preliminary stages will far be trumped by the advantages it will deliver for the company in the long run.

Chapter 19: Sustaining the Gains from Lean Manufacturing

Lean manufacturing is becoming a popular and widely used set of techniques and approaches aimed at boosting profitability and increasing competitiveness among major companies worldwide.

Because the world economy has somehow been subjected to various crises and turmoil from political and other economic hurdles, companies around the world are currently on the receding trend.

That is why companies do acknowledge the importance of integrating within them and adopting the helpful and effective strategies and principles of lean manufacturing.

Since lean manufacturing is basically involved in obtaining the right things, putting them to their proper and right places, during the right time, at the same time in ample and sufficient quantities, companies adopting them should really be careful in implementing them.

Lean manufacturing fundamentally aims to reduce waste and make companies more competitive by helping them turn into flexible firms which are open and subject to positive developments, innovations and changes.

Hence, the real challenges faced by all firms adopting the lean manufacturing principles are those that revolve around how to sustain gains from lean manufacturing.

Gains from lean manufacturing

There are several identified benefits that can surely arise from successful and effective implementation of lean manufacturing principles.

It is apparent and logical to state that lean manufacturing can have positive, direct and immediate influence and impact on companies. Implementation of lean manufacturing measures and techniques will surely and undoubtedly bring about numerous and significant gains and benefits to companies.

Lean manufacturing is sure to get companies reduce or slash manufacturing time without sacrificing output number and quantities. Experts believe that by implementing lean manufacturing principles within operations, companies can have a 50% to 90% reduction in overall manufacturing time.

That gain from lean manufacturing can be sustained only by continuing to implement effectively the helpful and effective principles of lean manufacturing.

Space gains

Another gain sure to be brought about by effective implementation of lean manufacturing is the reduction or lessening of floor space requirements.

Because lean manufacturing also involves the effective and strategic elimination of wastes and unproductive equipment in the work place, companies are expected to maximize space, making worker freer and faster to move around the work stations.

That could be sustained by preventing to buy unnecessary equipment. Redundancies and duplication of machines" purposes and intent should also be avoided.

Increased benefits

If lean manufacturing reduces manufacturing time and floor space requirements, it can, on the other hand, increase a number of gainful aspects.

For one, productivity of companies increases by using and adopting the lean manufacturing principles and techniques. As mentioned earlier, because disruptions and unnecessary wasteful machines are taken out of the work place, personnel are freer to move around.

The comforts given to employees make them more efficient and thus make them produce more outputs. In turn, that could be to the advantage of the company.

That lean manufacturing gain can be sustained by maintaining the smooth and effective implementation of lean manufacturing strategies and techniques.

Other gains of lean manufacturing

Companies adopting and integrating lean manufacturing techniques in their operations are also expected to improve their overall customer and client focus, boost the leadership potentials of their key personnel and make up for a leaner structure of the business.

What benefits would it be if companies achieve these gains? Of course, the overall profitability, competency and image of the company will be significantly boosted.

That would really count amid an intense competition, hard economic environment and overall rising of operational costs among companies.

To sustain such gains, it would be really imperative for companies to really maintain their focus on their goals and priorities upon implementing lean manufacturing techniques and principles.

Companies should remember that reaping benefits from such strategies upon initial successful implementation should not be a guarantee that the gains would keep on pouring.

Strong will power and determination would really keep companies afloat and surviving. Sustaining gains would be as hard an activity as seeking profit improvements and boosting competitiveness, but it is one concept and aspect, companies should really strive to get into.

Chapter 20: Advantages of Lean Manufacturing

Lean manufacturing is the processes, techniques, strategies and initiatives being implemented by companies around the world that aim to reduce unnecessary and unproductive tasks, activities and behaviours in the work environment.

Because the times have really gone hard, demanding and intense due to political and turbulent concerns affecting all nations, firms are currently facing challenges to be able to keep their profitability and efficiency.

Lean manufacturing not only reduces operational costs but also targets to boost, restore and significantly raise the competitiveness of a company.

There are seven identified "forms of waste" within the work environment and systems that lean manufacturing principally aims to alleviate, if not totally eliminate. These are over production, over processing, transportation, motion, inventory, waiting and scrap and defects.

Several advantages of adopting lean manufacturing principles

The first advantage identified by experts from implementing lean manufacturing techniques and strategies is the reduction of manufacturing time.

95

When the manufacturing lead time is significantly lowered, it follows that the operational costs incurred from the use of energy, utilities and wages from labourers" time will also be significantly reduced.

Thus, lean manufacturing helps companies retain, maintain and significantly increase their earnings, widen their margins and help them generate savings from lower costs.

Space is another area where lean manufacturing advantages are clearly and effectively exhibited. Working space, it is understood, is one of the primary and basic factors that keep operations of businesses going.

Labour and human resource experts estimate that adoption of good and effective lean manufacturing techniques and strategies will likely help companies reduce their physical floor space requirements by as much as 5% to 30%.

The figures involved could be small and miniscule for your eyes, but, actually, that will significantly contribute to much more efficiency and savings. That would be an advantage almost all businesses will surely look after.

The advantage in productivity

It is found that in general, companies implementing and adhering to lean manufacturing practices significantly boost and increase their manufacturing productivity by as much as 75% to 125%.

It is because time and efforts are principally targeted by lean manufacturing processes. Thus, elimination of wastes, practices, behaviours and unnecessary and disturbing objects in the work place will surely and practically help workers get on to their tasks with much smooth pacing and comfort.

You know how it is when workers work without any distractions and interruptions. Productivity is very much maximized. Thus, lean manufacturing becomes a necessity for companies to be able to achieve that goal.

The advantages in terms of waste to profit relationships

It follows that elimination and reduction of wastes will gradually and efficiently help boost and raise up earnings and profits in companies.

Thus, elimination of wastes and unproductive activities, objects, tasks and behaviours in the work place will surely help the company and its personnel focus on the requirements and demands of the customer.

The advantage of that, above all is that, when customer satisfaction is achieved, sales will surely rise. The best way to establish a good relationship with customers is to improve the products and services offered to them.

Lean manufacturing would be of great help to achieve a good customer or client relations.

Another advantage brought about by lean manufacturing techniques among various companies and firms adopting it worldwide is streamlined, rationalized or lean structuring of the organization.

You should know that elimination of excess and unnecessary job positions and tasks in a company is a sure way to help that firm reduce labour costs and eventually lead to generate savings.

Lean manufacturing without a doubt brings that advantage of leanness upon organizations and companies practicing and adopting it.

Advantage on culture improvement

Various companies around the world are practicing and implementing different cultures. It is usually a cause of problems, conflicts and issues around and within the organization.

In lean manufacturing, the cultures are standardized, thus, unfavourable practices and behaviours of both the employees and the management are reduced, if not eliminated.

The greatest advantage of lean manufacturing in terms of cultures adopted by companies is that lean manufacturing makes the differences between management and personnel reach to a verging point.

Lean manufacturing principles should really be implemented by companies. It is high time to reap its advantages.

Chapter 21: Lean Manufacturing Led Signs

Lean manufacturing processes and systems have required the need for lean manufacturing LED signs or displays to be able to monitor and adjust the process flow within the business systems.

The principles and beliefs of the lean manufacturing system that was created by the Japanese have become accepted worldwide and have been so widespread that chances are a common layman could have heard something about it or are directly involved in some type or form of it.

The idea of lean manufacturing is that a business or company can divide its workforce into possible distinct processes or work cells that can be easily monitored and adjusted. These companies with an active lean manufacturing programs or systems have to understand the need to map and measure the every stage of their available value stream for each product or goods with the aim or objective of eliminating or reducing waste from every system or process.

The use of lean manufacturing LED signs will enhance a company's lean manufacturing programs. Using lean manufacturing led signs will quickly improve the effectiveness and efficiency of any existing lean manufacturing program by giving the business or company the ability to post the measurements exactly where they are needed most.

Some of the available lean manufacturing LED signs are the following:

1. The Alpha 7120 displaying plant efficiency data.
2. The Alpha 9240 displaying the overall shipping performance.
3. The Alpha Vision PC displaying productivity information.

Using lean manufacturing LED signs can help a company to achieve the following targets:

1. About 40% - 50% reduction in the cycle time
2. About 25% - 35% reduction in the set up time
3. About 35% - 45% reduction in the down time
4. bout 30% - 40% improvement in overall productivity
5. About 25% - 35% reduction in the WIP
6. About 35% - 45% reduction in the scrap
7. About 40% - 80% reduction in the travel distance
8. About 20% - 30% reduction in the floor space

Companies that are fully engaged in the lean manufacturing programs or systems needs to have lean manufacturing LED signs to be able to achieve results like these.

Key Lean Manufacturing Principles

Lean manufacturing define value precisely from the perspective of the end customer.

It identifies the entire value stream for each of the product line and eliminates waste.

Lean manufacturing makes the value added activities flow.

Lean manufacturing provides what the customer needs only when the customer demands for it.

Lean manufacturing pursues perfection through its continuous improvement.

The Cornerstones of an Effective Lean Manufacturing Program

To create an exciting culture. Using lean manufacturing LED signs will definitely create an exciting and dynamic culture.

To empower a participative environment. With the use of lean manufacturing LED signs, employees of business companies can readily participate in the continuous improvement of lean manufacturing processes and flows.

To provide and give meaningful visual measurements using lean manufacturing LED signs.

To organize a visual and orderly work environment. The use of lean manufacturing LED signs will promote the organization.

To encourage a continuous improvement of the learning environment. Using a lean manufacturing LED signs will promote a possible continuity of improvement.

What are Visual Workplace Solutions?

Manufacturing enterprises have thought about it. How much did they spend on various information systems or equipment just to create great and efficient reports that will be reviewed after the fact? The use of lean manufacturing LED signs will make the key elements of the various reports to be available to the employees or people that really have a need for them immediately or instantly.

With the purpose of supporting the key principles of lean manufacturing systems and programs, various manufacturers of lean manufacturing LED signs have produced a whole line or family of such lean manufacturing LED signs. These lean manufacturing Led signs are Visual Workplace Solutions or VWS that are designed specifically to be able to deliver key lean manufacturing performance metrics to the people or employees that requires them the most.

The lean manufacturing LED signs and displays are the performance scoreboards and indicators in order to achieve the impressive gains in a lean environment. Lean Manufacturing LED Signs Performance Scores and Metrics

A business or company must put the right data in front of the employees or the right people and will yield or provide instant and immediate results and will improve the people morale at the same time.

Chapter 22: Lean Manufacturing Towards Success

To put it simply, lean manufacturing espouses the 'no waste' philosophy in managing the workplace and production processes. It does not know any company size. Whether it is a major corporation or a small group of five housewives with a cookie business, successful lean manufacturing techniques lies in its implementation and the discipline of those participating in it.

Experts say that lean manufacturing first gained popularity in Japan; a country best known for its highly unique and innovative approaches to a variety of things and methods, even with problem-solving strategies.

Lean manufacturing principles border on the practical and the simple. But, again, while they can be easily understood and implemented, maintaining the right attitude all throughout is a different story.

Because of the success lean manufacturing has brought to the companies that adopt it, for instance, Toyota, firms are now seeking to apply the strategy to their own corporations.

It is a fact that all firms need to reduce costs, what with rising energy prices and intensifying competition. Reading business journals, you can see that firms are filing for bankruptcy left and right, citing mismanagement as the most common cause of the receivership in the UK and Chapter 11 filings in the US. Even the most stable companies have fallen prey to these. This is why lean manufacturing is starting to become the overhaul method of choice for firms wanting to get back on track.

Lean manufacturing is a holistic and innovative approach to making companies profits and earnings somehow upbeat and at par with contemporaries around the world.

Companies around the world, in all aspects and in all industries, are now addressing lean manufacturing issues and concerns, one way or another. The fact that all companies need to reduce operation costs and expenses make up to the companies ever enduring efforts and initiatives to adopt lean manufacturing principles.

Lean manufacturing is also helping companies around the world to cope up with the real and emerging challenges in the real world when prices and costs are so volatile and influential to modern living and economies.

There are more and more companies around the world that successfully implement lean manufacturing techniques and principles in their daily operation.

It should be noted that companies that use lean manufacturing with success are characterized by one and a single unifying feature all of them are profitable and strong.

Companies that use lean manufacturing with success are also notably very competitive amid intense and rising competition in the corporate world; therefore you should embrace lean culture in everything you do.

Chapter 23: The Toyota Lean Manufacturing System

The standard lean manufacturing system has been referenced from the Toyota lean manufacturing system in Japan. Even the lean manufacturing system developed in North America has evolved from its beginnings in the Toyota Production System (TPS) in Japan.

In fact, many of the recognized phrases being used in the lean manufacturing systems in North America and all over the world are Japanese terms such as kanban, kaizen or andon. These Japanese terms originated from the Toyota lean manufacturing systems and have become standard and normal terms in every lean manufacturing system available in every country.

The Heart of the Toyota Lean Manufacturing System

Value has been the heart of the Toyota lean manufacturing system. When we say value, it means something that a particular customer desires to pay for or even buy.

As such, if there is value, then there is also non-value in the Toyota lean manufacturing system. Non value is everything that is not of value, meaning all aspects of the Toyota lean manufacturing processes are considered a waste or of no value.

Basically, the Toyota lean manufacturing system has an objective to be used as a tool in focusing all resources or energies in producing certain value-added characteristics while also identifying, acknowledging and eliminating the activities that are of no value.

The Toyota Lean Manufacturing System

The Toyota lean manufacturing is a sort of codification of several ideas into a set of workable harmonies.

First, a company who adopted the Toyota lean manufacturing system must be able to identify a particular customer and how or what is value to them. Afterwards, the Toyota lean manufacturing system will be able to guide the companies and employees to focus their energies into adding value to the goods.

By delineating the existing manufacturing process to the demands of the customer, the Toyota lean manufacturing system will be able to add value to the products or goods. In the end, the customers, the employees and the shareholders of the companies will all be satisfied.

The Waste in the Toyota Lean Manufacturing System

The Toyota lean manufacturing system faces a hindrance in its aims to improve manufacturing processes. The waste has become the focus of the Toyota lean manufacturing system although it is taught that focus and energies must be directed towards the valued goods as wanted by the customers.

Previous manufacturing processes has defined and categorized wastes as objects. The teachings of the Toyota lean manufacturing system, however, expands this view into meaning that wastes are not only objects but can be processes of the manufacturing system.

The Toyota lean manufacturing system rather defines waste in terms of the relationship between the resource and the end customers. Anything therefore that is not of interest to the customer but incurs expense to the company is a waste for the Toyota lean manufacturing system.

Continuous Improvement in the Toyota Lean Manufacturing System

The Toyota lean manufacturing system is bent on pursuing continuous improvement for all its processes. Any redundant or looping process will have to be terminated or replaced to improve the manufacturing process.

The Toyota lean manufacturing system allows itself to be open and adaptive to any changes. By identifying what wastes exist in the value stream, immediate and instant gains are acquired and achieved.

The Plan of Toyota Lean Manufacturing System

The Toyota lean manufacturing system lays out a plan to increase the profitability of companies by reducing the costs that can be incurred. This is done by knowing and tagging what the customers identify as value therefore, any processes or objects that do not align with this value or do not add value to the object is reduced or eliminated.

When a company adopts the Toyota lean manufacturing system, it knows that it can direct cost savings by eliminating wastes in the system.

Using the Toyota lean manufacturing process, companies can readily see the following improvements in their company:

1. An increased morale and productivity of the employee.
2. Satisfaction for the customer because of reduced defects on the goods and an improved delivery.
3. The goods will also be faster to market.

As was said previously, the Toyota lean manufacturing system is very much customer focused.

Chapter 24: Lean Manufacturing 3rd Party Logistics

Lately, lean manufacturing is being implemented by companies by hiring third party logistics. Lean manufacturing by third party logistics is possible by outsourcing.

Lean Manufacturing by Third Party Logistics

Outsourcing is currently the trend in most businesses today. In fact, General Motors of North America has been using outsourcing as part of its competitive advantage strategies. This company has plenty of experience when it comes to the analysis of an outsourcing company's capabilities and solutions.

Lean manufacturing by third party logistics is being utilized by most of the companies today including General Motors. General Motors identified the Power train Warren plant where General Motors can implement lean manufacturing and they used third party logistics to do this.

It embraced lean manufacturing principles by third party logistics and used the plant to effectively manufacture engines. It also used lean manufacturing by third party logistics to resolve transportation issues.

Later general Motors decided to further use lean manufacturing by third party logistics for the entire group. Greater benefits are evident from the economies of scale. Clearly, the teachings of lean manufacturing are to add value and eliminate waste simplifying the manufacturing process.

Steps Done In Choosing Lean Manufacturing By Third Party Logistics

General Motors made its choice on what potential supplier or third party logistics to choose from a number of factors enumerated below:

1. The overall quality of the lean manufacturing by third party logistics.

2. The service of the lean manufacturing by third party logistics.

3. The available technology or innovation of the lean manufacturing by third party logistics.

4. The price of the lean manufacturing by third party logistics. The Benefits From Lean Manufacturing By Third Party Logistics

In line with the principles of lean manufacturing, the outsourcing party must be able to do it all in the least costly and the most relaxed manner.

The strategy of General Motors to outsource its transportation function has been very effective and is rather working well. The third party logistics have a 99 percent record for on-time performance and has met its objective to gain significant savings for General Motors.

The lean manufacturing by third party logistics has been implemented rather well in the case of General Motors. The available visibility of the products and data information via the supply chain pipeline of General Motors has been a value that was unexpected.

Furthermore, the lean manufacturing by third party logistics strategy covered scanning of all the General Motor's freight and updated the advance shipping notifications of General Motors.

To make sure that both parties will combine their efforts to continuously improve processes in line with the principles of lean manufacturing, the outsourcing arrangement will include a gain sharing component.

Lessons Available from the Outsourcing Journal

The lean manufacturing by third party logistics strategy is effective since outsourcing several of the company's functions such as the transportation functions will allow a buyer to possibly leverage the strength of the supplier in the economies of scale in order to be able to achieve a number of objectives that include on-time performance and cost reduction. From the view of the third-party logistics supplier, it will manage the transportation function. It may also decide on using subcontract arrangements for some portions of the route, or otherwise perform and deliver the transportation services along with the management decisive component.

Lean manufacturing by third party logistics have a gain sharing mechanism indicated in the outsourcing contract which is a highly effective option for an incentive as well as for continuous reduction of cost and the improvement of services.

Chapter 25: Lean Manufacturing Printing Industry

The printing industry, just like all other global industries, is also affected by the crunches and economic hardships affecting global corporate firms nowadays.

The printing industry is mostly affected now by the rising popularity of the internet. The broadcast industry, for the past few decades have dominated the whole media universe.

That is why when revenues of broadcast companies started falling in the past couple of years, people and companies around the world were taken in awe and disbelief.

Why? Because the present people, probably including you, have grown up sitting in front of the television. People in these times have grown and become TV addicts.

For decades, TV has dominated and taken most of the advertising revenues. The radio industry has taken the second pie of the chart and the printing industry the least market and advertising share.

Hard times for the printing industry

Obviously, the printing industry is the hardest hit by the emergence of the internet. The least ad revenue share once enjoyed by the printing industry is now made even smaller.

All the companies around the world are living out the hardest of all times today. The printing industry is sure the hardest hit by the popularity of the online media.

Revenues and profits of printing industry firms are significantly falling and declining. That is why every month, you probably are hearing or reading news about job cuts, mergers and acquisitions, bankruptcy and selling off of many companies that belong to the printing industry.

It is basically the hardest time for the printing industry. It is most of all made worse by the current economic events and problems that are not unique to the printing industry.

Lean Manufacturing

Companies from around the world, from all industries, are now adopting the techniques and principles of lean manufacturing.

Lean manufacturing refers to the set of strategies and techniques implemented in the work place that aim to reduce, significantly cut down, operating costs and expenses of companies.

There are seven identified wastes that lean manufacturing intends to eliminate in the work place. These seven are identified as: over processing, over production, motion, transportation, waiting, inventory and scrap and defects.

Each waste contributes to the losses the companies incur with much quantity. Quality of outputs of companies are also lessened and sacrificed. What is worse is that competitiveness is much affected also. Indeed, the prevailing time is characterized by the cliché 'survival of the fittest."

Lean manufacturing may be the last hope for the printing industry. Because of the promises, the forecast and expected savings companies can reap from implementing lean manufacturing principles. The printing industry is believed to be the most and primarily boosted and lifted up by the lean manufacturing approaches.

The printing industry has somehow turned into a damsel in distress. With the lean manufacturing, figuratively, its knight in shining armour.

The manufacturing industry is benefiting from the gains and advantages of the adoption of lean manufacturing techniques. The printing industry, obviously, will also have the same gains some experts believe there will be much more.

It is about time printing industries now implement lean manufacturing techniques on her own. For sure, lean manufacturing adoption will not make the printing industry outpace or displace the online industry. But one thing is for sure.

Lean manufacturing will surely help print industry players last and outlive its destiny. It is said that printing industry is not meant to last longer. It can be true because the time and technologies have evolved along with people's preferences and interests.

The printing industry surely needs its redemption factor. This is the opportunity it has been waiting all along. The opportunity to generate savings reduces operational costs and improves efficiency and competitiveness, all rolled into one single package. Lean manufacturing is the best means to lift up the printing industry.

Chapter 26: Lean Manufacturing in Steel Companies

Steel companies have caught up with the fever and are trying to implement lean manufacturing in their operations. Lean manufacturing of steel is a production process that seeks to eliminate waste in all steel production phases with the end purpose of satisfying the customer.

Results of a successful implementation of lean manufacturing of steel are monumental: huge reductions in production cost and inventory and cycle times, large gains in quality, and evident improvements in delivery reliability.

Traditional approaches to implement basic lean manufacturing in companies involve:

(a) A top-down rolling out of concepts

(b) Installing and following goal-curves across management levels, meaning departmental goals must be in sync with each other and people are held accountable to meeting their targets

(c) Doing the easy tasks first and gaining momentum from small successful results

(d) Interactive education and creating atmosphere that welcomes taking risks and

(e) Initiating a pilot project before wide scale implementation.

Although very worthwhile, lean manufacturing is a very complicated process by itself. Lean manufacturing of steel even creates unique problems.

Steel parts that carry loads like automotive trains, jet engines, industrial bearings and metal-forming machinery are produced in a time-consuming multi-step process that involves a lot of grinding and polishing.

Steel parts are first moulded out of metal that is relatively soft and then hardened by being subjected to high heat and quickly cooled in a liquid, or "quenched." After this, steel parts still require precision finishing processes to produce ultra-smooth surfaces that reduce friction and wear

In steel production, equipments are often physically huge that rearrangement of these to reduce unnecessary human and machine movements may be unrealistic. Some processes in manufacturing of steel must be performed in large batches.

Because of the size of the products made, cycle time is often longer than in other manufacturing businesses. Metallurgical constraints limit the aggressive acceleration of heat-up and cool-down cycles.

Difficult equipment set-up increase production time, effort, yield loss and equipment deterioration.

Protective inventories are necessary to avoid costly "out of metal" conditions during bottleneck operations and cannot be avoided. Traditional "kanban" or 'signal controls are not suitable because some mills have a variety of routings and passes on the same equipment.

Also, unions and uncooperative labour relations make empowerment of employees and team building difficult to establish.

Despite these drawbacks, there have been success stories of lean manufacturing of steel.

In order to slash manufacturing costs by up to 30 percent and as to add $6 billion to the U.S. economy every year, Edison Materials Technology Centre developed and refine, from 2000 to 2005, an innovative technique for making a wide array of hardened steel parts through lean manufacturing of steel.

"Hard turning", a method to forge hot metal into nearly perfect parts and hardening and machining these after, was discovered to eliminate waste and possibly the need for polluting oils which are used in cutting and grinding. If hard turning will be applied to manufacture gears and turbine blades, this would meet EMTC's goals.

EMTC has developed hard-turning technologies and a complete prototype system. Other members of the team are Delphi Automotive Systems, Torrington Co., Kennametal, Third Wave, Hardinge, Inc., Masco

Tech, Georgia Institute of Technology, and Ohio State University.

Applying lean manufacturing of steel, Cairns Steel Fabricators also doubled its capacity and improved productivity. Established in 1979, CSF is a company focusing on steel fabrication and erection which employs around 60 personnel and handles 150 tonnes of steel per week.

QMI solutions offered a holistic approach to lean manufacturing of steel through its ProEdge Manufacturing Excellence program.

To ensure lean manufacturing of steel, CSF decided to address its internal processes first before expanding. CSF altered factory layout, housekeeping and machinery setup. Efficient use of space and equipment resulted to increased productivity.

CSF positioned individual work areas in specific spots and colour-coded tools to ensure they are returned to their proper places. In CSF's case, it was important to look at the "little everyday things" in order to make the system leaner.

Chapter 27: Lean Manufacturing Certification

A Simple Checklist to Obtain a Lean Manufacturing Certification

Life around the world, even in the first world and fully developed countries has really gone very hard.

There are lots of concerns and issues that hound firms around the world. Unfortunately, these issues make companies" profitability and competitiveness at risk and declining.

Thus, experts, managers and human resources organizations have verged to come out with principles and strategies that are aimed at helping firms improve their earnings and keep operations.

Most firms now are starting to look at lean manufacturing to be able to keep with the changing and challenging times. Lean manufacturing principles are surely getting their way into various companies" door steps.

Lean manufacturing as a discipline is expected to stay, not just in the manufacturing industry, but also in all industries and sectors.

Insufficient implementation of lean manufacturing principles

The number of companies adopting lean manufacturing principles is surely and is apparently on the rise, no doubt about that.

But the thing is, firms adopting lean manufacturing techniques are most of the time, not achieving target and aimed results because they are not doing the strategies and techniques properly.

It is reported by experts and by some consultancy firms around the world that companies adopting lean manufacturing principles are most of the time not implementing across-the-board and significant progress.

These companies are found to not attain the performance and efficiency improvements they aim to achieve. It is like working out in the gym. If the form and processes of a person is not properly executed, he will only get tired but not achieve his desired physical result.

Insufficient and ineffective implementation of lean manufacturing principles and techniques will surely make the companies" efforts and capital infusion for the initiative futile and wasted.

Lean manufacturing certification

Because the problem of insufficient and ineffective implementation of lean manufacturing principles and techniques among companies are rising and rapidly concerning, organizations and experts around the world have agreed to set standards and gauge effectiveness of implementation of lean manufacturing principles.

To find out and determine whether companies are doing the right processes and techniques, and whether they are implementing maximized lean manufacturing techniques, industries gave come out with lean manufacturing certification program.

Lean manufacturing certification, just like any other standard check programs, categorize companies and identify those that are effectively implementing lean manufacturing techniques within their work systems.

Lean manufacturing is a sure way to make companies retain and achieve profitability. That is why; organizations and advocates feel bad if the targets and intent of the principles are not met. The primary aim of lean manufacturing certification program is to make sure the intent and purpose of lean manufacturing lived up.

A simple checklist for lean manufacturing certification

A company is expected to benefit and reap the advantages of lean manufacturing if its answers and responses to the following questions are on the affirmative.

Otherwise, the company should make sure it is qualified to get lean manufacturing certification by consulting experts and going through the whole process to make sure everything is done appropriately, properly and in the right pacing.

Here the questions companies should look into to review if they are qualified to get a lean manufacturing certification:

Is the performance improvement aimed at by your company upon implementing the lean manufacturing principles been achieved?

Is your company successful in applying and instilling upon workers the principles of lean manufacturing? Have the best practices been introduced and implemented?

Is the structure of the company been made lean and practical?

Are the target results that should come from the implementation of lean manufacturing techniques achieved?

Are there no more room for improvements, or is the company now enjoying significant cost reductions from improved efficiencies and streamlined operations?

Lean manufacturing certification assessments

Companies adopting lean manufacturing principles are usually assessed and evaluated by standard organization to determine whether they are qualified for lean manufacturing certification.

In doing so, the companies" performances are subject to specially designed scoring system. Lean manufacturing certification's scoring system is established to review if companies' measure up to high and world class standards and practices.

It is somehow similar to ISO, which has become, over the years, a standard quality assurance gauge in manufacturing facilities and businesses around the world.

Lean manufacturing criteria used to judge or assess companies adopting lean manufacturing principles are specially designed to allow experts and evaluators to rate and assign scores to the subjected companies.

Chapter 28: Lean Manufacturing Six Sigma

For the purpose of completeness, I could not bring this book to conclusion without comparing lean manufacturing to six sigma.

Both lean manufacturing and six sigma are management philosophies or tools that help a company eliminate wastefulness in manufacturing and other types of industry.

Because the times are changing, processes advancing and needs intensifying, more and more companies face challenges as regards their efficiency and profitability. And both lean manufacturing and six sigma introduce solutions to these dilemmas, without putting much strain on a firm's energy and resources.

Lean manufacturing

Lean manufacturing has been proven to significantly aid in the streamlining of operations and reduction of waste. It welcomes the concept of continuously raising the value added to a certain business activity or method via the reduction of the so-called seven wastes.

What lean manufacturing does is provide implementing firms with adequate tools to make it in the increasingly competitive global market, which is everyday faster turnaround times, higher quality and lower prices.

Here are some advantages of lean manufacturing:

- Lean manufacturing strengthens production processes
- Lean manufacturing significantly lower the chain of wasteful activities and resources
- Lean manufacturing increases flexibility by improving layouts - lean manufacturing reduces floor space needs and inventory dramatically, and
- Lean manufacturing introduces and implements more appropriate and up-to-date delivery systems

Six Sigma

The six sigma management philosophy, like lean manufacturing, is also tailored to reduce waste, but it is more focused on eliminating waste linked with production method or equipment defects.

The tools under six sigma are used by firms to further improve and develop a company's products and systems, via the consolidation of engineering, business and statistical data. As with lean manufacturing, six sigma can also be applied to any form of corporation or organization, whether engaged in the services, marketing, design, sales or production industries.

Some advantages delivered by the six sigma management tool:

- Six sigma improves and boost a firm's systems and products
- Six sigma reduces the chain of wastes
- Six sigma lessens costs by around 50% via self-financed methods
- Six sigma easily adapts to changer customer tastes
- Six sigma drives growth using the internal resources available to it

What both philosophies do is help firms dramatically increase their productivity by around 75% to 125% because they ensure that no time, energy or resource is wasted in any of the processing levels. To put it in simple terms, both lean manufacturing and six sigma are bent on nipping problems at the bud, or, even nipping problems before they occur.

A vigilant approach to business is what companies need nowadays to be able to cope with the fast changing times. Sure, while some systems have worked for us for decades now, it wouldn't hurt to try something that is relatively new and proven to be so much better at delivering positive results.

Chapter 29: Conclusion

Lean manufacturing is a set of strategies and business approaches that help firms attain the desired level of profitability and competitiveness.

Lean manufacturing are applied in manufacturing facilities that aim to maximize their earnings capabilities by boosting production, maximizing labour resources and reducing expenses and costs.

The key to the success of lean manufacturing is effective implementation and religious adherence to the principles contained in the set of the strategies. Lean manufacturing principally targets companies" expenses.

By lowering companies" costs and operational expenses, lean manufacturing serves its purpose and use. That is considered the key to achieving all of the companies" goals and targets.

Reducing costs leads in generating savings and preventing further negative losses. You know that companies need to lower or trim down their expenses to be able to attain their goals and put up the target profits.

Facilities and lean manufacturing

Lean manufacturing are implemented particularly and especially in facilities and plants where outputs are the principal concern. Because outputs in these facilities are the principal drivers of revenues and income, companies are very keen to maximize their human resources to attain a target level of output production.

Manufacturing companies are very much keen to save on costs. In that regard, lean manufacturing principles and strategies become very helpful to them.

Companies around the world suffer from crunches brought about by the prevailing economic conditions. Because political and energy crises affect and infect the world, companies are becoming more and more keen and anxious to implement innovative and effective techniques to minimize costs.

That is when lean manufacturing sets in. When companies need to improve efficiencies and generate significant costs, they turn to lean manufacturing strategies.

An effective and religious implementation of lean manufacturing techniques can lead to the success and survival of a business organization or company. How? Through the savings and improved level of competitiveness, companies" profitability are boosted.

Planning for lean manufacturing implementation

Before implementing lean manufacturing principles and techniques, it will be advisable for a firm to first conduct initial and intensive planning.

Just like when companies are engaging in significant and major projects and initiatives, planning is an important factor in successfully implementing lean manufacturing strategies and principles.

Planning involves the initial consideration and review of the major business aspects and areas that could be affected by the implementation of the lean manufacturing principles.

Planning in lean manufacturing involves the careful and thorough study of the whole facilities and plants that would be covered by the initiative. Lean manufacturing will be more of a success if effective and realistic planning initiatives are first conducted before the final and sure-bet implementation stage.

There are a number of human resources specialists and consulting firms that offer services pertaining and involving lean manufacturing. Even in your locality, for sure you can find these consultants that could help your business.

Costs are inevitable. They are part of the capital and investment requirements in the business. That is why lean manufacturing principles are mostly implemented by companies in their manufacturing facilities.

Reduction of costs and a boost in competitiveness will surely lift up a firm, especially during these dire times, when even a single cent in savings means a lot to companies.

It is recommended that before your company embark on a lean manufacturing initiative, it should first address some concerns and make specific and realistic planning to make the implementation of lean manufacturing schemes really work.

If you need help on lean manufacturing training or implementation, feel free to contact us via this link. http://www.improvenetprofit.aaglobalsourcing.com/contact

Good Luck!

www.ingramcontent.com/pod-product-compliance
Lightning Source LLC
Chambersburg PA
CBHW051713170526
45167CB00002B/637